Reflections In God's Great Outdoors

Reflections In God's Great Outdoors

John Quinn

All rights reserved. No part of this book may be reproduced, stored in a retrieval system, or transmitted in any form, or by any means, electronic, mechanical, photocopying, recording or otherwise, without permission of the author.

Copyright @ 2015 John Quinn

ISBN-13: 9781516846665
ISBN-10: 1516846664

Cover Photo by Charles J. Alsheimer
Used with Permission

DEDICATION

This book is dedicated to you and every outdoorsman that wants a deeper relationship with our Lord and Savior, Jesus Christ

Contents

	Foreword	ix
	Acknowledgements	xi
Chapter 1	The Mask	1
Chapter 2	Obsession	4
Chapter 3	Lone Ranger	7
Chapter 4	Are You Talking to Me?	10
Chapter 5	Well Done!	13
Chapter 6	Captivated	16
Chapter 7	Heavenly Soap	19
Chapter 8	The Mirage	22
Chapter 9	The Stranger	25
Chapter 10	Hooked	28
Chapter 11	The Sword	31
Chapter 12	The Forty Five Second Break	34
Chapter 13	The Brotherhood	37
Chapter 14	The Predator	40
Chapter 15	The Armored Vest	43
Chapter 16	Camouflage	46
Chapter 17	Hunter 0 Turkey 1	49
Chapter 18	Lost!	52
Chapter 19	The Legacy	55
Chapter 20	Who Is Calling Please?	58
Chapter 21	The Reach	61

Chapter 22	The Adventure	64
Chapter 23	The Flushing	67
Chapter 24	The Whiff	70
Chapter 25	The Sanctuary	73
Chapter 26	Weapon Ready?	76
Chapter 27	Bread Crumbs	79
Chapter 28	The Fall	82
Chapter 29	Watchful	85
Chapter 30	Wounded	88

Foreword

I HAD CONTEMPLATED WRITING THIS book for many years but never thought it was the right time. Then one day I felt and sensed a great presence of the Lord and almost a voice saying that now was the time. Timing is everything when the Lord is involved so I sat down and began to write. I had always had a desire that the Lord would use my passion for hunting and fishing to reach others for Him and not just for my own enjoyment. I went back through my mind for various adventures, misadventures and observations I had experienced throughout my hunting and fishing outings. I felt that each one had a spiritual application that we as hunters and fishermen and women could understand in our world. Most of the applications are from personal experience, some good and some painful. Some are from simple observations I have made while sitting in a stand.

It would be my desire that each devotion would be used to draw us closer to Him. I wrote each one as the Lord directed me to write. Some are very direct warnings of areas of our lives that God wants us to guard. Others are meant for those that are struggling and need encouragement. As I looked back at the variety of messages contained throughout the devotionals I realized that God was wanting to challenge us in our walk with Him.

The days are over that we should take our Christianity lightly. Any type of Christian value in this country is disintegrating at a furious pace. Church doctrine that at one time was based on Biblical principles is now based on political correctness. The church is under attack and that means that we are under attack.

The devil, our adversary, senses that the end of time as we know it will come to an end soon. And therefore has stepped up his attack on individuals that make up the church. These chapters are not about feeling good and life as usual. It's about a real in-depth look at our relationship with Jesus.

I trust that as you read each chapter, you will take a few minutes and examine your walk and ask God if there is anything that may need changing. I want this devotional to be used as a tool that we take a closer look at ourselves and our walk with Jesus. My utmost desire for this book is that we will have an even greater desire to release the things that hold us back so we can draw closer to Him. Let our lives will be changed for His glory!

John Quinn

Acknowledgements

I wish to thank first and foremost my Lord and Savior Jesus Christ for His great love and mercy He has shown me.

I am also thankful for the desire He has placed in my heart to enjoy the beautiful outdoors He has created for us to enjoy.

I wish to thank my wife Heidi for the encouragement and drive she has given me to write this book. I am also grateful for her understanding of my love for the outdoors and the many hours I spend in them.

I am thankful for my hunting and fishing partner, Rodney, that has taken this once novice outdoorsman and taught him how to hunt and fish and enjoy the outdoors.

I wish to thank my friend Garland, who is now in the presence of the Lord. He was a man of great faith that God placed in my life to help me understand the depth of God's love and forgiveness.

"Let the fields exult and all that is in it,

Then all the trees of the forest will sing for joy

Before the Lord, for He is coming."

Psalm 96:12, 13 NASB

"Let the rivers clap their hands,

Let the mountains sing together for joy

Before the Lord, for He is coming

To judge the earth."

Psalm 98: 8, 9 NASB

CHAPTER 1
The Mask

*"The prudent sees the evil and hides himself,
But the naïve go on, and are punished for it."*

— Proverbs 22:3 NASB

It was the spring of 2007 and after many years of unsuccessful turkey hunting, I was out again in pursuit of my first spring gobbler. I was still in the learning curve but didn't realize at the time that I would be in that curve for most of my turkey hunting life. I love the idea of turkey hunting. I enjoy watching the early morning sunrise with the woods waking up and the birds singing their morning songs. Squirrels are beginning to scurry making your heart beat faster as you begin to wonder if perhaps a turkey had somehow snuck up behind you. You don't even blink as your eyes scan the woods around you. I love that early morning coffee from my faithful thermos that is always packed away in my backpack. Then suddenly you hear the sound of the king of the spring woods, the majestic gobbler.

I was hunting on private ground that day in a turkey rich area of Western Maryland. Around midmorning I heard the worst sounding hen call I had ever heard coming from the top of the small hollow I was sitting in. At first my thoughts wondered what hunter would ever try and make such a horrible sound and expect a turkey to come and investigate. Then I realized I was on private ground and no other hunter should be on this land but also understood that it was not my property. The owner certainly had a right to allow anyone to hunt here and I was privileged to be at least one of them. And so I waited to see what would unfold here.

A few minutes later I noticed movement in front of me coming over a small knoll and saw the head of a turkey suddenly appear. I believed it was in fact the hen I had just heard minutes before. Apparently she had not watched the DVD's on turkey language. I had my decoys set out in a small clearing and she passed not more than 30 yards to my right and eventually passed behind me and out of sight. I thought this would be a good natural set up if a gobbler came by. The decoys were in front of me and the real hen behind me. And again I waited. Not more than a few minutes later I noticed movement from the same area that the hen had just came from. Over the same knoll I see the head of a gobbler coming and he notices the hen decoys. He turns suddenly and heads straight for the decoys and I am thinking this could be the day for my first gobbler.

Now this next statement will explain what is about to happen. I wear glasses and that particular morning was cold so I put on two facemasks to protect my face from the cold. Do you see what's coming? I saw the gobbler coming and in the excitement I got over heated. When that happened my glasses began to fog up and I couldn't see anything. So ever so slowly I begin to reach up to pull one of my face masks down. Did I mention ever so slowly? Ever so slowly was not enough and the gobbler notices the slight movement and I hear the putt-putt and he is gone as quickly as he came. And actually probably twice as fast as he came. What do I feel now? From the high anticipation of what I thought might happen to the low of total disbelief and defeat. I'm sure many who are reading this have been there before.

Reflecting back on the actions of the turkey, I have realized a spiritual truth that we can apply to our lives. He saw and sensed danger and immediately left the area. He didn't play with the danger nor was he interested at all in finding out what the danger was. He didn't think that he could somehow handle it, he just left. How many times do we see danger and sense the Spirit warning us but we continue on towards the danger instead of turning away. And too often, we reap the consequences of not following the Scripture's admonition. As you reflect on the turkey's actions, is there something that God is warning you of today?

Dear Lord, Help me to be sensitive to Your leading as You try to keep us from walking into danger. Give me the courage to walk away in spite of the often beautiful but deadly enticement. In Jesus Name, Amen.

CHAPTER 2

Obsession

"As the deer pant for the water brooks,
so my soul pants for You O God."

— Psalm 42:1 NASB

ONCE YOU HAVE BEEN BITTEN by the outdoor bug, it often manifests itself in erratic and unusual behavior. You caught your first big fish, you shot your first deer or you called in and killed your first turkey. Something happens in a person's brain that is similar to a stadium light being turned on in a small dark room. A whole new world has just opened up and a person cannot get enough of it. You go home from that outdoor adventure and you read everything you can find about that subject. You order magazines, buy DVD's and start attending sports shows and attending seminars related to that particular interest.

When I shot and missed my first turkey, I came home and read everything I could find on why we miss turkeys. I actually missed him twice as he gave me a second shot, all to no avail. After the heartbreak of disappointment, I asked myself, "How could I have missed?" Was it just poor shooting? Turkey fever? Pride? I actually discovered the number one reason for first time turkey shooters is not having your cheek tight against the stock of your gun. That alters the line of sight and will almost always cause a miss as it did for myself.

This episode reminded me of the time I came back to the Lord after many years of chasing the wrong things. I couldn't get enough of reading books on how to get closer to the Lord and how to know Him better. I was obsessed!

A more balanced and consistent approach might work better here but I just couldn't get enough! Reading the Bible on a daily basis and spending time in prayer is perhaps the best way to learn more about the One who loved us enough to give His life for us. Attending a local Bible believing church and being a faithful attendee will help you to get to know Him more. There are more books written by a variety of godly authors than you could read in your lifetime. Books that have been written to help you know and understand Him more and give you guidance on living a God-centered life. Asking your Pastor or some godly friends would be helpful as well. There are CD's and DVD's on living a Christian life and Christian music that is available. As we grow in the knowledge of the Lord we begin to understand the depth of the love that Jesus has for us. Once we begin to understand that our lives begin to truly change.

This past spring I was fortunate enough to harvest two gobblers. I have been reading everything I can to know and understand the wild turkey even better. May I never forget however to continue to grow in the knowledge of Him. The Bible states, "You will seek Me and find Me when you search for Me with all your heart, I will be found by you, declares the Lord." Jeremiah 29:13,14 NASB. Remember that God certainly wants us to enjoy the outdoors that He created for our enjoyment but He also wants us to pursue Him with an even greater desire.

Dear Lord, Thank you for the passion You have given us to hunt and enjoy the beautiful outdoors You have created. Please give me a greater hunger and passion to know You most of all. In Jesus Name, Amen.

CHAPTER 3

Lone Ranger

"And if one can overpower him is alone, two can resist him. A cord of three strands is not quickly torn apart."

— Ecclesiastes 4:12 NASB

I was sitting in my stand late one evening watching chipmunks scurrying here and there. Not much deer activity this evening but every rustle of a chipmunk in the dry leaves brought me to attention as they can sound like a deer approaching. The smell of autumn is in the air and you can feel the coolness as the sun begins to disappear over the mountains. In our area, as with many, the deer move through these woods right before dark as the sun begins to set and the shadows move out. The final twilight hour sharpens your senses in anticipation of any final deer movement and one last draw of the bow before the night settles in.

Then suddenly I see movement through the brush and the deer are making their way up from the creek bottom. There is a natural trail they follow when they do come through here and tonight is the night. I see the first one make the turn at the bottom of the hollow and begin to make her way up the trail. Then a second, third and finally the fourth deer, all does, heading up the trail to the twenty yard spot below my stand. My breathing has become a little heavier and the anticipation is making my heart beat more rapidly than normal. I grip my bow and my arrow release is already attached to the D loop on my string. Now I wait for an opportunity while I try and calm down and settle in and let my instincts take over. When two are feeding, two have their heads up constantly scanning for movement and the danger that can come with it.

As a bow hunter, it is hard to pull the arrow back and make the angle corrections when two sets of eyes are watching you. They may have already noticed something amiss in the tree you are in. Not enough to sound the alarm but enough that it would take one errant blink of an eye to send an explosion of snorting deer running everywhere. I would rather have one single deer come in, put it's head down to feed or look away from the stand to prepare to take the shot.

That is why God wants us to stay in fellowship with other believers. Together we can watch out for each other and warn the other when we see danger coming that perhaps they didn't. We make an easy target for the devil when we try to do it alone as the Lone Ranger Christian. It just never works. While we might engage in certain, perhaps questionable activities or maybe even legitimate but not necessarily uplifting activities, we have no one looking out for danger and no one watching our backs. A lone deer is an easy target when no one is watching for him. It doesn't work well for them and will not work well for us either.

Becoming a member of a local Bible believing church is a good way to get plugged in to godly fellowship. In addition you can attend Bible studies, go on hunting or fishing adventures with Christian friends and develop a core group of trusted friends. If you have not become a part of a local fellowship, may I encourage you to do so as soon as possible. Do not become an easy target for the enemy. You can make the devil, our enemy, as frustrated as the bow hunter that says, "I will never be able to get to that one as long as all those others are hanging around warning him."

Dear Lord, Help me not to think that I can make it on my own and to realize the power in fellowship with other believers. May I also be a watchman for others. In Jesus Name, Amen.

CHAPTER 4

Are You Talking to Me?

"My sheep hear My voice, and I know them, and they follow Me."

— John 10:27 NASB

I AM ALWAYS AMAZED AT the wildlife you see while hunting. I've always said that you won't see that kind of stuff sitting on your couch watching TV or playing video games. I was on my stand one morning when I noticed movement. Out of the brush came a sow black bear and her two cubs. The two cubs lingered below my stand while momma bear watched from around forty yards down the hollow. Finally one cub left to go with momma and they started to walk away. The remaining cub lingered and I wondered how far momma and the single cub would go until junior decided it was time to leave and go with them. The woods were very quiet that morning and you could hear most anything from a long way off. Momma and the other cub finally stopped around 60-70 yards away. I didn't hear any communication between momma and the cub that lingered but it was obvious the cub did. Suddenly the cub's head snapped up and it whirled around like a top and began to run to her momma and its sibling. When junior finally caught up, the three of them ambled off together.

I am not a bear biologist but the scene that played out that morning told me that there was some kind of communication between momma bear and her cub. And while I didn't hear anything verbal, the cub obviously heard something and knew it was momma bear. The cub heard and recognized her voice and followed her.

And so it is when God speaks to us. I know He loves the entire world but more specifically He loves you, and He loves me. And if He loves me, He knows how to speak to me so I can recognize His voice. And if I am spiritually perceptive I am able to hear His voice and respond accordingly. The Bible states that Jesus said, "My sheep hear My voice and they follow Me." John 10:27 NASB. He may speak to others in a different way but He knows how to speak to each one of us so we know it is Him speaking.

Others may not hear or perceive that He is speaking to me but I will know. God speaks to us in a variety of ways. He may speak directly from His Word, the Bible during our reading sessions with Him. He may speak through godly people and that person may not realize that God just used them to speak to me. But I know exactly what God was saying to me. At other times He speaks directly into our heart and soul. Once we learn to hear His voice we then need to decide to follow the advice or commands that He has given us. He can warn us of danger, give us direction or feelings of peace or dread that tells us that the situation is not from Him. If we train ourselves and allow Him to help us, we will hear His voice and like the bear cub, make our head snap to attention and whirl us around to help us follow Him through our own path through the woods of life.

Dear Lord, Help my heart to know that when You speak, I know it is You and then help me to follow. I know You will lead me and guide me as a shepherd does for his sheep. Help me not to stray and to always stay within the sound of Your voice. In Jesus Name, Amen.

CHAPTER 5
Well Done!

"For am I now seeking the favor of men, or of God?"

— Galatians 1:10 NASB

We all, or some of us, want to be the superhero that saves the city or the world from the massive spaceships from another planet and their alien life forms. We are then given the key to the city and elevated to a position of prominence, given the Hero Medal of Valor and a joyous reception from a grateful nation. After all, everyone loves a hero! Okay, so maybe we don't really want to be the hero.

Maybe there is another pedestal we want to be on in a more 'realistic' world in which we as hunters and outdoorsman live. We practice, we study, and we scout, all to find the biggest buck or to catch the largest fish. After all, it takes a very skilled hunter or fisherman (or woman) to do these great feats. Not just anyone can do them and it's mostly true, those that put the time in very often get rewarded with the very sought after prize. We might even get our name and picture in the outdoor section of our local newspaper. We want people to know what a great and successful hunter or fisherman we are. And I am not saying that we shouldn't be proud of our accomplishments. We do however enjoy that ten minutes of fame we receive and hear people say "We sure are proud of you, you are a great outdoorsman (or woman)." And we gladly accept the accolades. Is all of this wrong? Certainly not, if we stay humble and grateful in the process.

But there is still another arena in which we live that we should strive to receive accolades. The Bible states that we should "Be diligent to present yourself approved to God as workman that does not need to be ashamed, accurately handling the word of truth." 2 Timothy 2:15 NASB.

So the question we need to ask ourselves is that do we engage ourselves in the pursuit and study of God's Word so that we would be approved to God? I pursue hunting with a passion as I'm sure you do as well. But I do read repeatedly in God's Word that we should be feeding the hungry and taking care of the orphan and widow. Are we engaged in these activities or other activities that God's Word has shown us that are important to His heart?

He has created this world for us to enjoy, including the animals and fish we pursue. He has also put in many of us the DNA that gives us to desire to pursue these activities. God loves us and wants us to be happy and enjoy our time on earth, to which I am thankful. In the end however, who caught the biggest fish or who killed the biggest buck will not really matter. While our time on earth we need to strike a balance between the things God has given us to enjoy and the things that contain more eternal consequences. What will really matter is to hear the words, "Well done, good and faithful servant." Matthew 25:23 NASB. These are the words of accolades that we really want to hear!

Dear Lord, Help me always to recognize the approval of You is more important than the approval of men. Help myself and others to see by my actions that Your approval is the most important thing in my life. In Jesus Name, Amen.

CHAPTER 6

Captivated

*"...in order that Satan might not outwit us.
For we are not unaware of his schemes."*

— 2 Corinthians 2:11 NLT

The first gobbler that I killed was in the spring of 2013. It was an unbelievable feeling that after all the years of 'almost' there was finally a gobbler on the ground. That surreal feeling that you almost feel like it is a dream but you can feel yourself standing there. I had heard this gobbler down below in a field and hoped he might follow a known pattern of running this ridgeline up to the flats that overlooked this field. I worked my way far around the property that would bring me to the top of the ridgeline and I would set up there and wait. I gave him some time and called a few times with no response. So I gave him some additional time and he finally gobbled once. He was working his way up the ridgeline, just as I had hoped he would. If he continued this line of travel he would come out at the top of the ridgeline where I had set up with my decoys. Then I saw him slowly making his way toward me and he would pass in front of me around 20 yards. He didn't put on much of a show as far as turkeys normally do. He went in strut with a full fan for a brief moment and continued in. He got to the decoys and stared at them but he just didn't seem relaxed. He started to nervously look around, head going up and down and back and forth and turned away like he was getting ready to leave. He seemed to sense that something just wasn't right. He delayed a few more seconds and I quickly realized that now was the time to take the shot. My 12 gauge shotgun roared and down he went.

Feelings of exhalation and intense relief from the disappointments of many years and tears began to flow. Yes, real men do cry. Maybe not at a romantic movie but we do have emotions, although directed in strange ways. Was I an expert turkey caller that put him down? No, certainly not. I did play out some strategy that paid off but I don't believe that was what killed him. What I do believe killed him was his unwillingness to listen to that voice in his head and his desire to linger in the face of danger. He was obviously nervous from the moment he got close to the decoys but wasn't sure what to do about it, at least not in time anyways.

Just a few more flirtatious words, listen to a few more inappropriate jokes, one more look at something inappropriate on the computer monitor, one more 'white lie', just one more, one more, I can handle it you say. You told yourself that to justify your actions but know in your heart it was wrong. Your heart was beating fast and you felt this impending feeling of wrongness but you were captivated and perhaps held by the lure of sin. Much like the turkey that sensed something was wrong but unwilling to get away fast enough. He lingered, and then he died. King David, in 2 Samuel, Chapter

11, watched a woman named Bathsheba bathe on her rooftop. From all of his exploits that God had helped him with, David certainly knew this was wrong but still he lingered. You can read the entire story but he eventually took her, the wife of a soldier that had been sent away to fight a war. And David paid a very severe personal toll for that encounter. Let us resolve to run away from danger as soon as the Holy Spirit begins to nudge us and save ourselves and perhaps our families from the "...sin that so easily entangles us..." Hebrews 12:1 NASB.

Dear Lord, Help me to be aware of the schemes of our enemy that would tempt us to sin. May the Holy Spirit give me the power to run from sin so I don't hurt myself or those I love. In Jesus Name, Amen.

CHAPTER 7

Heavenly Soap

"Let us strip off every weight that slows us down, especially the sin that so easily trips us up."

— Hebrews 12:1 NLT

I WILL ADMIT THAT I am a fanatic about scent control when I am hunting. I will go to great lengths to be scent free when I enter the world of the whitetail deer. I am an avid bow hunter and my ideal shot range is 20 yards so that is where I set my stand from any trail that deer are using. With a whitetail's nose so ultimately more sensitive than a human's, perhaps more than 200 percent greater, it becomes obvious why I feel the need to be scent free. In my many years of hunting I have consistently been within 15-20 yards from deer in my stand and as long as I don't move, they have not detected me, at least that I am aware of. I have had deer walk directly under my stand and walk a trail 15 yards downwind of me and didn't scent me.

Let's begin with hand washing all of my hunting clothes with unscented detergent and hanging them to air dry. Once dry, they are immediately put in a scent free clothing bag. This washing includes underwear, socks, base layers, hats, gloves, balaclava, outer clothing and any other clothing articles. I wipe down all of my gear with unscented wipes that includes my bow, arrows, arrow release, quiver, watch, flashlight, knives, boots, etc. I also don't wear my outer hunting clothing to and from the hunt as they are kept in an airtight, unscented bag. Once I get to my hunting area I use an unscented odor killing spray to coat all of my clothing again right before I journey from my vehicle. The bottom line is that I do not want one ounce of the smell of the 'world' on me when I enter the world of the whitetail and alert them to my presence.

There is also another area of fanaticism that we need to be concerned with that has further reaching consequences than just having a whitetail deer smell us. And that is my desire to cleanse my spiritual self of any contamination of the world as well. That contamination is simply called sin. The Bible states that "You shall be holy because I am holy." I Peter 1:16 NASB. We are admonished again and again to rid ourselves of sin and are told by Jesus that while we are in the world but we are not of the world. We should therefore not act like the world but rather try to imitate the life of Christ. We must also understand that we don't have righteousness on our own but our righteousness is found in a relationship with Christ. That does not mean that we can lead a reckless life without regard to the life Christ desires for us, which is a holy and godly life.

We need to take some time in our quiet moments with the Lord and reflect on how much of the 'world' continues to hang on us. During that time we can ask God to reveal anything that needs to be let go. We must understand that we are not perfect and will stumble on occasion but we must continue to strive and move forward for a life that is pleasing to God.

It stands to reason that if we are so conscious of carrying our 'world' into the woods and the enjoyment that brings to us as hunters, should we not also be equally if not greater concerned of carrying our 'world' into our spiritual lives that will have everlasting consequences? Are there things that we are carrying that we need to 'wash' with heavenly soap?

Dear Lord, Please examine my heart and reveal to me anything that is not pleasing to You. Help me to cleanse myself of these things so my life can be a true reflection of You. In Jesus Name, Amen.

CHAPTER 8
The Mirage

"For where jealousy and selfish ambition exist, there is disorder and every evil thing."

—James 3:16 NASB

I DECIDED TO TRY SOMETHING new one October morning during our bow hunting season and set up a doe decoy. It was a one dimensional decoy with a painted picture and looked fairly realistic from a distance. I had hoped to draw in a buck close enough to get a shot. The decoy was around 20 yards from my stand but not exactly where I wanted to place it due to some windy conditions. Around 8:00 that morning I sprayed some doe in estrous from an aerosol can into the wind that blew from right to left that morning. It drifted through the hardwoods where my stand was and into a thicker group of trees and brush. I then did a few grunt calls and out of this thicker group of trees a nice little six point comes trotting straight toward the decoy like he was on a string. Everything so far was working according to plan.

He stops right behind a tree without offering me a clear shot and then steps into the shooting area. Instead of going directly to the decoy he decides to circle slightly around to come in from the right side and behind the decoy. That meant he was coming directly in front of me and would pass by the stand around 10 yards out. I had no cover in this particular tree and thought if he makes it to the thick group of saplings directly to my right and circles the decoy he will see that he has been duped and take off. I knew that drawing the bow this close without cover is not an ideal situation and that he might see the movement when I drew the bow. I was hoping he was still focused on the decoy. It was either try and probably not get a shot at all so I went ahead and drew the bow.

Well, as you can probably guess, it turned out not to be the best decision I would make that day as he saw me draw and decided to leave. He didn't snort or bolt, he just knew something wasn't just right as he walked away. Even though he came into this situation looking for something else, he was smart enough to know that if he continued when something inside his brain told him not to, the outcome would not be a good one. His decision was a good one and that day he lived.

Sometimes as Christians we see things not as they actually are but how we would like to see them, much like the deer did. The deer realized this almost too late but the fact that he acted on his ultimate suspicions was a lifesaver for him. We like to think that the grass is somehow 'greener' on the other side of the fence. A new wife, a new job or a different church all can appear as what we would like them to be rather than what they really are. In some cases, they are just sinful acts that have no basis or justification in the Word of

God. Others are just poor, carnal led decisions that will not work out the way you would like them to. Do you really think that a new church is going to solve all the issues you had at the last church? Do you think the next church is somehow the perfect church you always knew existed? Do you think the relationship with the new wife will end up living 'happily ever after'? You thought that last time. We used to hear stories of people lost in the desert and under a delirious mind reached out to the lush, watered oasis only to grasp a handful of sand. That's very similar to what can happen to us if we are led by carnal desires.

Dear Lord, Help me to be Spirit-led in my decisions and not moved by every wind of doctrine or every greener grass I see. Help me to be content in You and Your plans for me. In Jesus Name, Amen.

CHAPTER 9

The Stranger

"...and came to him and bandaged up his wounds...
and brought him to an inn and took care of him."

— Luke 10:34 NASB

I was hunting with friends in the Savage River Forest in Garret County in Western Maryland. It is steep rugged terrain fit for goats and not the faint of heart. I was with perhaps the most diehard hunters I have ever hunted with. We would be out before daylight and back after dark, up and down hollows and mountainsides that I would look at and think, "Surely we are not going up there?" In a few minutes we were in fact "going up there!"

We were on a deer drive and I was assigned to be one of the drivers and not the standers so I was on the move. On the very last leg of my part of the drive, perhaps within 20 yards of the stander, I slipped on the icy granules that had formed that cold morning that resembled frozen ball bearings. I went down so fast that I didn't even realized I had fallen until I felt the intense pain in my right wrist. It quickly swelled to twice its size and twisted in an unusual way. To say I had never felt that kind of pain before would be an understatement. From the look of it, it was certainly broken in a very bad way. The stander saw me fall and radioed to the other hunters what had happened and help was on the scene quickly. The pain became so intense I nearly passed out.

Kevin, the leader of our band of brothers arrived and began to help set the wrist to prevent further damage. He found a thick stick to use as a splint and began to wrap it with electrical tape. One of the other hunters suggested I bite on a bullet because he said it might hurt when he wrapped it. I suggested to him that he had watched too many westerns but realized I might in fact need something to help. I suggested a stick which helped tremendously as the pain was nearly unbearable. After immobilizing the wrist I was told to sit on the ground until they assembled my gear and we would head down the mountain together. Now understand that I had laid on the cold ground what seemed like an hour so I was cold and decided to try and stand up. What I didn't realize that one of my legs had fallen asleep and while I tried to stand, I began to fall over like a tree that had just been chopped and nearly fell down a steep ravine. After being reprimanded I stayed on the ground this time. We successfully made it down the mountain to safety and I was driven to the emergency room at our local hospital. I was eventually put in a cast from fingertip to armpit for six weeks!

We all need friends to come alongside us sometimes to help us walk out of a bad situation. It may have been self inflicted or it may have been circumstances or inflicted by others. It reminds me of the story of the Good Samaritan that went out of his way to help a total stranger. He was on his way to somewhere but saw someone that needed help and decided to help him, regardless if it was an inconvenience to him. And he was a total stranger to the man that was hurt. If a brother has fallen or even a total stranger that needs someone to help, we need to be aware that we all need help at one time or another. Has anyone ever gone out of their way to help us? Then certainly we need to do the same for others. If we see someone in need, let's not assume that help is already on the way. Maybe God was sending you!

Dear Lord, Help me to not be so busy that I cannot stop to help someone in need. I don't want to just learn about love but I want to show it by my compassion and actions to others. In Jesus Name, Amen.

CHAPTER 10
Hooked

*"...each one looking to yourself, so that
you too will not be tempted."*

— Galatians 6:1 NASB

One of my great warm weather passions is fly fishing. There is just something magical about it that I can't really describe. Maybe I just like doing things the hard way because the greater the challenge, the greater the reward kind of thing. It is just you and the fish. Generally there are no onlookers to cheer you on or to suggest doing this or that, unless you are with a friend and then it is allowed. A fish does basically three things during his life. He swims, he eats and he avoids predators. So when a fish does this 24/7 he tends to get pretty good at it.

Now enter the fly fisherman with a vast variety of flies, as they are called, in his or her fly box and trying to find the right fly to what is called 'matching the hatch.' This is just a fancy phrase for just trying to find what the fish are eating at that moment in time. It gets very technical from that point so we will just leave it there. We try to find a fly that will be enticing to that particular species of fish. I fly fish for trout so I am looking for just the right fly that I think the trout will take a fancy to. After spending a lot of time in rivers and streams over the years, you gain a certain amount of knowledge that you will use to entice a fish to come up and take hold of the fly. Sometimes you get it right, more often not, but it's the chase we love. We try to figure out what fly to use, where we think the fish are laying in the water, what is the best way to approach the fish so as not to scare them and the whole expectation of actually getting it right.

Then we watch that 'perfect' fly float down the river, over the area we think the trout will be and suddenly the water explodes as the fish comes out from beneath the water, takes the fly, you set the hook and the game is on! If our hooks are sharp and we keep just enough pressure on the line, the fish will be unable to spit out the hook and we are then able to successfully land him in the net. We have actually become the predator in the life of a fish but the grin on our face shows that we are happy with that accomplishment.

There is another predator on the loose and we are his fish in the river. We have become the fish that are trying not to get caught. The devil, our adversary, is said to be roaming the earth looking for someone to devour. Now he doesn't present himself as ugly and mean and looking like he wants to kill us, but he does. He, like the fisherman, knows what kind of enticement to use to make the catch. And he has studied you and knows your addictions and weaknesses. He knows exactly when you are the weakest and knows exactly what kind of 'fly' to use. And when he does, if we are not aware of his dealings, we will take the fly, which is called sin, and we are caught. His hooks are always kept sharp and he knows how to keep pressure on so you will not get loose until we land in his net. Oftentimes our 'net time' will bring pain and destruction to ourselves and those we love. God does forgive us but the damage has already been done.

Let us be aware of his schemes and be spiritually discerning to know when one of those has been placed in our path. Like many fish that I go after, let us refuse that fancy fly and swim quickly away to our Heavenly Father.

Dear Lord, Help me not to fall for the schemes of the enemy of our souls. Let my life be one of integrity and righteousness and one that is pleasing to You. In Jesus Name, Amen.

CHAPTER 11

The Sword

"You have placed our iniquities before You, Our secret sins in the light of Your presence."

— Psalms 90:8 NASB

I love to hunt for the whitetail deer with my bow. There is just something exciting about the whole experience. My comfort range is 20 yards so to be able to get that close to a deer and actually get a shot takes a lot of work. The preparation process for me starts long before the season opens. I need to have confidence in every piece of gear that I use. If it's something new I purchased, I need to field test it before I can take it on an actual hunt. The clothes need washed in unscented detergent and placed in airtight, scent free bags. All my gear needs wiped down with odor killing wipes including my bow and each arrow. I try to leave nothing to chance. At 20 yards, you don't normally get a second one. I spend plenty of time at the range in my backyard with the bow. Every arrow is spin tested and individually shot to ensure accuracy. Each arrow is then put in the quiver in order of the exactness of their accuracy. When the opportunity comes to take a deer, I want the broadhead to be sharp, accurate and be able to make a clean efficient strike in the kill zone. In the anatomy of the deer, an accurate arrow will pierce the heart and lung area and cause a quick death.

Interestingly enough, in the world of the hunting arena, the arrow and broadhead cause death but in the spiritual world there is a sharp weapon as well but it produces just the opposite effect. This weapon is in fact a two edged sword and equally adept in causing a major wounding in the heart of man, but the wounding that results in not death but life. The Bible states that the "…Word of God is living and active and sharper than any two edged sword and piercing as far as the division of soul and spirit, of both joints and marrow, and able to judge the thoughts and intentions of the heart…" Hebrews 4:12 NASB. As we are exposed to the Word of God, whether in a local church fellowship, by Christian friends or in our private devotions the Word of God can speak to us. It tells us that "While we were yet sinners, Christ died for us." Romans 5:8 NASB. That means that even in our sinful state, God loved us enough to send His only Son, Jesus Christ, to die for our sins and take the punishment that we rightly deserved. We would have spent eternity away from the presence of God without the sacrifice that Christ made. When we discover that and repent from our sins and ask Jesus to come into our hearts, death has been changed into not only life, but eternal life with Him.

For us Christians, known or unknown sins become exposed and repentance will bring us back into a closer relationship with the Lord. My own experience has shown that during those moments when the Word of God pierces our heart, we can literally feel like our physical heart has been pierced. At that point we become nearly unable to move as the guilt of our heart is revealed. As we repent, God in effect removes the sword and we realize that even through the sins, God never stopped loving us and has now provided a way for us to be forgiven. Take a moment and ask God to search your heart and allow the two edged sword to reveal to you anything that needs cleansed from your heart.

Dear Lord, I willingly ask that You reveal and expose any sins that I have in my heart that are hindering my relationship with You and others. Please forgive me of these sins and help me so no sin has dominion over me. In Jesus Name, Amen.

CHAPTER 12

The Forty Five Second Break

"...and a time to laugh..."

— Ecclesiastes 3:4 NASB

For most of us, hunting is serious business. We plan and prepare meticulously and with a certain amount of luck thrown in, we are successful in the field. We walk softly to our stands and often without our flashlights on. If we do speak, it is in whispers so the game will not hear us and be alerted. The bottom line is that we are prepared and are deadly serious. But if we spend enough time in the field, funny things are going to happen. One of those lighter hearted moments I was recalling happened many years ago but was so funny, we still laugh about it today.

I was hunting in Clearfield County, Pennsylvania during the late muzzleloader seasons with my then father-in-law. It was cold and damp on this particular December day. We had decided that I would be a stander while Sonny would circle around and try and push some deer my way. It would take him awhile to get into position so I decided to sit down on the damp ground against a tree and wait. Being a cold morning I had my morning coffee and probably a little more than I should have. Cold, damp mornings and coffee are not a good combination for me and there is a reason why I never drink it during bow season before a morning hunt. Because of the extended length of range for a shot with a rifle or muzzleloader, I usually take some liberties with the morning coffee drinking. I would soon find out that was a liberty I should not have taken that morning. Due to the excessive coffee I had drank that morning, I finally had to get up and relieve myself. I laid my muzzleloader against the tree and stood up an arms length away to take care of business. They say timing is everything in life and it certainly held true that morning. After all the waiting I had done, I picked the wrong time to take a forty-five second break.

Right in the middle of this much needed break, I heard an awful commotion coming through the woods and looked up to see an entire herd of deer heading straight for me at a very high rate of speed. I looked at them, looked at my gun, then looked back at them and feeling totally helpless to do anything about it. This was the moment I had been waiting for. As they hurled through the woods from one predator straight toward another, I could see the lead deer's eyes were as big as saucers. Her ears were laid back as she and the others stiffened their legs as they tried to dig their hooves into the frozen ground in an effort to stop. I finally recovered enough to grab the muzzleloader and get off a shot but at that point with their current rate of speed and now deer running everywhere, a machine gun would have had a hard time keeping up with them. A second follow up shot also failed to find its mark as I stood there with a smoking gun and deer still running in every direction.

When my father-in-law finally showed up he asked if I had shot and had I seen all the deer come through here. I said yes, I had. "Well" he said, "why didn't you shoot one?" All I could do was laugh and replayed the story for him. That was many years ago and while much has changed, we have stayed friends and when we get together, we often recall the story and have a good laugh together. The Bible states that "A joyful heart is good medicine." Proverbs 17:22 NASB. Hunting is serious business but always take a moment to recall the lighter moments you have had in the woods with your family and friends. These can be some of most memorable hunts!

Dear Lord, Help me to enjoy the great outdoors that You have made. Help me not to be so serious that I forget to laugh and make memories with family and friends. In Jesus Name, Amen.

CHAPTER 13

The Brotherhood

> "Brethren, even if anyone is caught in any trespass, you who are spiritual, restore such a one in a spirit of gentleness."
>
> — Galatians 6:1 NASB

Here in Maryland we have a Jr. Hunt Day that occurs one week prior to the opening day of our rifle season. The youth hunt with rifles but we can hunt with our bows on that day but we do need to wear the legal amount of blaze orange. My friend's nephew had a youth with him on the private land we hunt. I did not see a deer that day nor did my friend who was also bow hunting. Right before dark we both heard a shot in the area where the nephew and the young man were hunting and we had hoped that perhaps the youth had a deer on the ground.

As my hunting partner and I met at the four wheeler for the ride out of the hollow, we heard what we thought was a dog barking down the hollow in the area where we had heard the shot. We thought it was odd that a dog would be down this far in the hollow. Odd until we heard the rest of the pack start up and realized it was coyotes, not dogs. Coyotes are frequent visitors in the woods and hollows we hunt. We then wondered if indeed a deer was down and the coyotes might have found the carcass before the hunters did. On the way out of our hunting area we met up with his nephew and found out that the youth had shot a deer that had taken off down the hollow close to the area where we had heard the pack of coyotes. A search party was quickly assembled to go and quickly retrieve the deer before the coyotes did. If they hadn't already found the deer the coyotes may have smelled the blood and were in the process of assembling their own search party.

As hunters we respond quickly to another hunter who needs our help. After all, it's all part of our hunting 'brotherhood.' We wouldn't think about leaving one of our hunting party who may need help getting his deer out, maybe lost or alone in the woods. If he doesn't rendezvous at the appointed time we quickly respond and help.

Yet it seems odd that in our churches today we don't seem to have that same urgency to help our fallen brother or sister. We don't see a person or a family for awhile and we seem to be too busy with our own lives to find out what's happened or we don't want to violate their privacy. If a buddy called us late one night and said he had shot a deer but couldn't locate it and needed our help, chances are most of us would drop what we were doing and go and help him look, no matter how late.

On the spiritual side, maybe a brother got into trouble with an affair or some other self inflicted wound and we think it was his own fault and he or she will have to deal with it. We don't make any effort to reach out and see if we can help lead them back out of the darkness to where they need to be and help restore them. Maybe they are just too embarrassed to come and seek help yet are truly repentant for something that happened. Take a moment and think of someone that might need a call. Chances are they will be glad you did and so will you.

Dear Lord, It is only by Your grace that we can experience Your mercy and forgiveness of our sins. While we were sinners You still reached out to us. Help me now to reach out to others that may have fallen and need help to find their way back to You. In Jesus Name, Amen.

CHAPTER 14

The Predator

"so that no advantage would be taken of us by Satan, for we are not ignorant of his schemes."

— 2 Corinthians 2:11 NASB

It is uncanny how sharp the eyes of deer can be. During turkey season I was sitting on the ground against a tree in complete camouflage with the fake leaves and they could still pick me out from 100 yards away. Turkeys with their keen eyesight don't seem to see me but the deer sure do! As an avid bow hunter, it is imperative that we get above the line of sight of the deer. It is also good for any slight movement we need to make while drawing the bow. In addition, our scent can drift away above the deer's keen sense of smell. There are obviously many reasons we need to be in a treestand during archery season.

The bottom line is that we have become the predator, watching and waiting for an unsuspecting deer to walk by. If we have done our homework, we know the trails and times deer come through this section of woods. We also know what they like to eat and we know where their food source is. We know what makes them nervous and afraid and we know how to tempt them with scents and lures. We know nearly everything there is to know about our prey. And once the deer come walking under our stand and linger for a moment, we unleash our arrow and death may occur soon after.

This reminds me of another predator with similar knowledge and motives. The Bible states, "Be of sober spirit, be on the alert. Your adversary, the devil, prowls around like a roaring lion, seeking someone to devour." I Peter 5:8 NASB. We must always be on guard and alert to the schemes of the devil. He is out to destroy us in any way that he can. In fact Jesus said in John 10:19 that ""The thief comes only to steal and kill and destroy." He knows where you live, he knows what can tempt you and he knows how to strike a vicious blow that can literally destroy you, your family, your business or your church. He has studied you and he knows your habits and where you work. Does this all sound familiar? He is watching and waiting from his own treestand so to speak. Waiting for you to walk by where he has set a trap for you. He has laid out the scents and lures that he knows you will respond to. If we are not careful and always on the alert we will fall into that trap and death will certainly follow.

God has given the deer amazing eyesight, incredible hearing and extremely sensitive sense of smell to avoid danger. We as hunters are often able to overcome those lines of defense and harvest a deer. The devil has great abilities to overcome our defenses but only if we allow him to. The Bible states, "Greater is He that is in you than he that is in the world." I John 4:4 NASB. That simply means that we have greater resources than the devil living within us through the power of the Word of God, prayer and the Holy Spirit that will warn us of danger. Stay grounded and stay sensitive that we can see the devil's schemes and maintain our integrity before God, our families, friends and our church.

Dear Lord, Help me to be aware that there is a real enemy of my soul that is out to destroy me and those I love. Help my mind and heart to be alert at all times so I can guard myself and others of the attacks of the predator. In Jesus Name, Amen.

CHAPTER 15
The Armored Vest

> "Stand firm therefore…and having put on the breastplate of righteousness…taking up the shield of faith with which you will be able to extinguish all the flaming arrows of the evil one."
>
> — Ephesians 6:14,16 NASB

It was the second Saturday of our spring gobbler season here in Maryland. Opening day the week prior found me on private ground at the same tree I had taken a gobbler the year before. Not hearing any gobbling the first week I decided to check out a field down below me before I left. There was a turkey on the far end of the field but I couldn't tell what kind it was and it wouldn't respond to any of my calls. I decided the following week I would set up just inside the tree line and put my decoys out around 25 yards in the field. It would take me additional time to get down to the field and possibly walk under some roosted gobblers.

So the following week I left home with plenty of extra time for the new set up. All was going well as I pulled up to the parking spot and got dressed in my turkey gear. All I had to do was put on my turkey hunting vest and I would be off to the field. As I reached onto the back shelf of my van where I kept the vest I realized in near disbelief that it wasn't there. I searched through my large clothing bag in the hope that it was in there somewhere but I came to the shocking realization that I had left it at home on a hanger in the basement. All of my calls, strikers, gloves, balaclava, facemask etc. were in my vest. I was 30 minutes from home and that would put me an hour behind and all of the extra time I had allotted. I was already thinking of Plan B which would be to discard Plan A. I knew I had no choice but to return home and get the vest regardless of which plan I would use. I went home as quickly as I could and called ahead to my wife to let her know I would be going in the basement door so she wouldn't think someone was breaking in. I retrieved my vest and quickly returned to the hunting area. It was still dark so I decided to try and do the original set up. It did eventually end well as I took a gobbler that morning right after sunrise.

This story reminds me of the admonition from the Bible that states, "Put on the full armor of God, so that you will be able to stand firm against the schemes of the devil." Ephesians 6:11 NASB. Every day we get up and get dressed to go to work, school or just face the world at large. Some are meticulous, shoes shined, ties match the shirt, and skirts match the blouse along with the shoes and jewelry. We want to look our best!

But we forget that somewhere out there is our adversary, the devil, who is looking to deceive us and wants to kill and destroy us and our families in whatever way he can. He will inflict wounds and damage to our hearts that will have tragic consequences. Let us always remember that every day we need to put on the full armor of God so we can stand against our adversary and be able to stand firm against his advances in our lives. Think of it as a spiritual Kevlar vest and his schemes and the damage he does as bullets that are shot at us. As we immerse ourselves in the Word of God and prayer, we will have our armor on each and every day. I may have forgotten my vest but may we never forget to put our armor on!

Dear Lord, Help me each day to put on my spiritual armor and to realize that there is a real battle for my soul. Help me to stand firm and resist the devil for Your glory and honor. In Jesus Name, Amen.

CHAPTER 16
Camouflage

"You adulteresses, do you not know that friendship with the world is hostility toward God?"

—James 4:4 NASB

I admit that I am a brand specific camouflage junkie. It is a major brand camouflage and just about everything I have for hunting has to have it. There are others patterns that work exceptionally well but somewhere along the line I got hooked on this particular brand. I have consistently been within 10 to 20 yards of deer and they have not seen me which I attribute in a major part to the camouflage. I have confidence in it and I know it works for deer as well as for turkey hunting. I know it totally blends in with the surroundings whether it is in the brush on the ground or in the trees. Camouflage is an important part of our hunting experience as it helps us blend in with the surroundings. Without it we stick out like something that certainly doesn't belong in the woods and puts our prey on high alert.

Unfortunately that is the attitude that many Christians have taken into their world as well. They are called 'camouflage

Christians.' They hide their faith and blend in with the world to the point that most of their friends probably don't even know they would consider themselves Christians. Perhaps for fear of being ridiculed or maybe wanting to say something in a situation but fear of not being able to know what to say. We have all been there so this is not a judgment of any kind. We are told "Do not love the world nor the things in the world. If anyone loves the world, the love of the Father is not in him. For all that is in the world, the lust of the flesh and the lust of the eyes and the boastful pride of life, is not from the Father, but is from the world." 1 John 2:15,16 NASB

In our country being politically correct is the current wave and seems to be gaining momentum. That means that saying something that stands up for God's word is going to label us as 'haters.' Even many of America's churches are crumbling under the weight of being politically correct and setting aside very clearly defined Biblical positions on issues. This is clearly going to make speaking out even more difficult but we cannot remain silent. We must know what the Bible says on these subjects and be able to clearly quote the Scriptures with conviction to refute the liberalism that has spread through our country.

This is not the time to put on our 'camouflage' and say nothing. At times we will be hated for what we say but the Bible already told us, "Do not be surprised, brethren, if the world hates you." I John 3:13 NASB. In fact Jeremiah had already tried to keep from speaking about the Lord when he said, "But if I say, I will not remember Him, or speak anymore in His name, Then in my heart it becomes like a burning fire, Shut up in my bones. And I am weary of holding it in." Jeremiah 20:9 NASB. Do we need to be a preacher on a soapbox? No, but we do have a sphere of influence of family and friends. You might be surprised that you are not the only one that feels the way you do, they were just hesitant to say something. Let us take off our camouflage and ask God to give us the courage to speak out!

Dear Lord, Help me to be a voice for You in a dark and dying world. Despite heavy opposition I want to be a light to others and take a stand for righteousness regardless of the cost. In Jesus Name, Amen.

CHAPTER 17

Hunter 0 Turkey 1

> "Casting all your anxiety on Him,
> because He cares for you."
>
> — I Peter 5:7 NASB

I love turkey hunting. There is something so intensely challenging about it that it can become addicting. I have come to discover that there is nothing more heart pounding, breath taking and knee weakening than seeing a gobbler in full strut heading for the decoys. Knowing that you may have a chance to take a shot at a gobbler just puts goose bumps up and down your entire body.

I think that knowing at any moment, the slightest movement, the slightest noise or tiniest gleam of a piece of equipment can put an end to the hunt in a second. Everything has to be working perfectly on your part but there are so many variables outside of your control that can also put an end to the hunt in a hurry. That is probably why it is so challenging.

I will have to admit however, it wasn't always this exciting for me. I have hunted these birds for many years with the score always hunter 0 and turkey 1. One year I had two shots at the same turkey and missed both times. He was confused after I shot and missed and probably couldn't believe he was still alive. He looked around and walked slowly away so I shot again and missed again. I had a lot to learn back then and still do. I have spooked them and sent them running for their lives. I have had them come in gobbling but stop short of my gun range and also just walk by out of gun range. I have even walked over a knoll and come face to face with one. You can guess who won that little skirmish. And so it went on like that for many years. Yet I always looked forward to the next spring gobbler season. I approached each season with renewed optimism thinking that this would be the year it would all come together. It usually didn't but finally two years ago it did all come together. I bagged my first gobbler! As I was standing there looking at that first turkey on the ground it seemed like a surreal moment. I thought that day would never come but I never gave up.

So let this be an encouragement to you that God has not forgotten you. Perhaps you have been called to a ministry and you have struggled and not seen the results you envisioned. Maybe you have not found that career that you spent your college years training and preparing for. Perhaps Mr. or Mrs. 'Right' has not come by yet and you wonder if you will spend your life alone. You've struggled to make ends barely meet. Or maybe you have been going through the divorce or death of a loved one and struggles never seem to end and you are ready to just quit. Jesus told us. "I will never desert you, nor will I forsake you." Hebrews 13:5 NASB. These are not just lightly spoken words but a direct statement from His heart to yours. Spoken for the right time for you to grasp this truth.

He actually saw where you are now when He spoke those words.

God's promise to you is found in Jeremiah 29:11, NIV, "For I know the plans I have for you,' declares the Lord, 'plans to prosper you and not to harm you, plans to give you hope and a future". Don't quit and don't give up. He is standing beside you whispering your name and asking you to trust and follow Him.

Dear Lord, Please help me to know that sometimes life doesn't always work out the way I planned or hoped. May I still understand that You love me and that You still have a plan for me. Help me to be patient while I trust in You. In Jesus Name, Amen.

CHAPTER 18

Lost!

*"For the Son of Man has come to seek
and to save that which was lost"*

— Luke 19:10 NASB

Have you ever been lost? I mean really lost with no way out? I remember a hunt I was on in the Savage River State Forest many years ago but remember it today like it happened yesterday. I was fairly new to the area and myself and seven others were doing deer drives high in the mountains. Savage River State Forest is comprised of a total of approximately 55,000 acres of rugged, rocky mountainous terrain. It is segmented in parts but contains large areas of continuous forest land and is easy to get lost in, as I was about to find out. I was directed to be one of the drivers and was given directions and set out on my way. Due to the very large terrain we would be covering, drivers were not in visual nor verbal contact by radio. We were expected to keep our bearings and meet up at a certain location. I was situated on the outside of the drivers and therefore would not have anyone off to my right in the event I got turned around. Turned around would prove to be an understatement. To make it simple, I got lost and I mean lost in the middle of a very large forest. Every hill and valley all looked the same and eventually wasn't sure what direction I was headed in. Panic and fear gripped my heart. Do I hug a tree as we are told to do or continue and hope I run into one of the other drivers. I decided to press on. I walked for a long time without seeing or hearing anyone. My fellow hunters must know by now that I was not at the appointed meeting spot and being a rookie then, probably lost. I continued to wander with hope that somehow I would get out of this.

What seemed like several hours or more, I eventually came to a farmhouse and with great relief walked up to the door and knocked. The owner answered and I explained my predicament and told him where I was supposed to meet up with my fellow hunters. He simply replied, "You need to be where?" with a look of disbelief on his face. I asked which way it was and he replied that it was too far to walk back and offered to drive me there. At that point I realized just how lost I had been. Finally reunited with my hunting partners was a very humbling moment as this rookie outdoorsman realized how much he still had to learn.

And so it was when I didn't know Jesus Christ as my personal Lord and Savior. I really didn't realize how lost I was until a friend very gently with love, pointed out what the Bible said about going to heaven. I was religious and thought I could do it on my own. If I could be good enough and follow the church's doctrine everything would turn out great, or so I thought. What he showed me was that I would actually have to admit that I was a sinner and unable to redeem myself. I was eternally lost without asking Jesus to forgive me of my sins and ask Jesus to come into my heart.

If you have never made a decision to accept Jesus into your heart and have been reading these devotionals with some interest, please take some moments to search these Scriptures. Ask God to reveal His truth to you about what His Son did for you. You will be glad you did. (John 3:16, John 14:6, Ephesians 2:8,9). NASB.

Dear Lord, I understand that I am a sinner and that You came to earth to die for my sins. I confess these sins to You and ask that You come into my heart, forgive me of my sins and help me to start a brand new life with You. In Jesus Name, Amen.

CHAPTER 19

The Legacy

"For the report of your obedience has reached to all."

— Romans 16:19 NASB

As hunters and outdoorsman (and women) we seek for signs of the animals we pursue. For deer we are looking for fresh tracks and pellets which show that deer have used this particular trail with any consistency. We also look for well worn trails that indicate travel corridors. I may not have actually seen the deer but I know they have been there by the sign they have left. The tracks often leave an imprint of their being there. If we are looking for signs of turkeys we look for feathers and their distinctive shaped pellets as well as tracks in the mud. We also look for scratching in the forest floor that indicates that turkeys have been feeding and which direction of travel they were heading. I may not have seen the turkeys but I know they were there. Often the memory of that deer or turkey is hanging on our wall. It could be a full head mount, antlers on a plaque or mounted turkey fan. Or it might simply be a picture with a big smile on our face. We look at them and recall the details and excitement of the hunt. They become etched in our memory to recall at any time.

So naturally I begin to think how I will be remembered when I am gone. How will I be eulogized at my funeral? Have I left any tracks anywhere? If someone sees a picture of me hanging on a wall, how will my interaction with people that I loved and care about be remembered? Perhaps you have heard the poem of the dash in relation to this. It is too lengthy to print here but you can do a computer search for the entire contents. In essence it is a reminder of a person's life between the dates of birth and death. There is normally a dash between these dates and our life is remembered by what we did in the 'dash'.

Several years ago I spoke at the funeral of a close friend named Garland, a very godly man whom I highly respected. At a time in my life when I was undergoing some very personal challenges, it was this man, in the words of wisdom and encouragement he spoke, made me realize that my life still counted. My life was never the same after that and a deep healing began in my heart that may never have started without him. Garland left very deep tracks on my heart. Occasionally I will see the funeral card in the flyleaf of my Bible and I think of him and the impact he had on my life then, and even today.

I may be remembered as a successful hunter or fisherman but will that really matter at the end of my life? I hope to be remembered that I made an impact of people's lives and that people sought after God from words or actions that I did. I hope I was a reflection of His love during my 'dash' on earth. Will I be remembered as a man of integrity and a man of faith? Was I a man that loved his family and friends and encouraged them to be all that God wanted them to be?

So when people see your name in the obituary column, what will they think? If someone is invited to speak at your funeral, what do you think will be said? It's not too late to make a difference in someone's life for Christ. Ask God what you can do and He will guide you to the people He wants you to touch with His love and compassion. As Garland did, you might make an eternal difference in someone's life.

Dear Lord, When I leave this earth to be with You, may I be remembered as a man or woman of integrity, one whose actions reflected a love of Jesus and one who wanted to make a difference in people's lives for Christ. In Jesus Name, Amen.

CHAPTER 20

Who Is Calling Please?

"My sheep hear My voice, and I know them, and they follow Me."

—John 10:27 NASB

We love our animal calls. There are calls for every conceivable animal we are trying to draw in close for a harvest. If you have not used one you really should give it a try. We've seen them on the outdoor hunting television shows but I can't say that mine works as well as theirs do. When these hunting personalities make a deer grunt call, the deer seemingly come running like on a string just begging to be shot. Every turkey call they make a turkey responds with a gobble. Even if they don't work exactly like we see on those shows, I know for a fact they do work and I am fascinated with them.

There are deer grunt and bleat calls that work well during the rutting time in the fall. There are elk calls to bring in the big bull elk during their rutting period and predator calls to bring a coyote running across a field to finish off what he thought was a wounded rabbit. I especially like my turkey calls. There are slate calls, box calls, push button calls, glass calls and mouth calls. All sound a little different and all work to bring in the gobbler. I probably have more turkey calls than a turkey hunter could ever use in a lifetime. It's almost an addiction but when we pick up a new call and make the sound we are just sure this will be the one that will bring in the boss gobbler. And the challenging part is to make the call sound like the animal that we are pursuing. They hear a voice calling to them and they respond very often to their demise and find a place in our freezer.

I was amazed the first time I had a doe come below my stand when I made my first bleat call. The doe left a group of other does that were farther down the hollow and came up and looked around to see where the deer was. She didn't end up in the freezer as it was buck season but the fact remained that it worked. I've had bucks come in to the grunt call and gobblers come in to the hen call as he thought he was going on a date.

There are a lot of voices calling to us out there as well. A lot of them sound sincere and very convincing. Come here and go there, that's where your happiness lies. You don't need religion to tell you what to do, it's your life, be happy and do what you want to do. Come to our religion, there you will find eternal peace and ultimate rest. The Bible is just a book and it's outdated. God is love and He wants you to be happy.

The fact remains that Jesus said it very clearly when He said,"I am the way, the truth and the life, no one comes to the Father but through Me." John 14:6 NASB. So regardless of what we are told, Jesus Himself said the way to gain entrance into Heaven is through Him. Secondly, in Ephesians 4:14, NASB, we are told, "…we are no longer to be children, tossed here and there by waves and carried about by every wind of doctrine, by the mockery of men, by craftiness in deceitful scheming.". May I encourage you to read and study the Word so you know what you believe. Then you will know if a voice other than the voice of Jesus is calling you. Paul wrote to Timothy a message for that time and it is quite applicable for today as well. "… in later times some will fall away from the faith, paying attention to deceitful spirits and doctrines of demons…" I Timothy 4:1 NASB. May I encourage you to hold fast to the Word of God without wavering and listen only to the voice of our Lord.

Dear Lord, While there are many voices calling me today, let my heart and mind be alert to hear Your voice. Let me never be deceived by those that claim to know You, yet proclaim a message contrary to Your Word. In Jesus Name, Amen.

CHAPTER 21
The Reach

"A wise man is cautious and turns away from evil."

— Proverbs 2:19 NASB

Fly fishing is a fun but challenging sport. It is all about waving a stick while standing in a river trying to catch a fish. It's a little more complicated than that but that is how it appears to the general non fly fishing person. It often entails going into deeper water that we probably should be going into because the fish we want are almost always on the other side of the river. At least that is what happened on this trip.

I just knew that a fish would be behind this large boulder across the river waiting for food in the form of a mayfly to drift by. So the natural thing to do was to go after it. So I waded out and was so focused on getting just a little closer that I didn't realize how deep the water was getting or how strong the current had become.

When I did get focused on my situation instead of focusing on the fish I realized I was in a bad spot. The water was then above my waist. The current was starting to push me down the river, and I had both feet on the bottom. It felt as if

I was skiing underwater. I started to panic and remembered that the number one rule for wading in a strong current is not to lift a foot off the bottom of the river. This move would offset any balance I may have, as delicate as it may be, and cause me to be pushed over. In as deep of water as this was, that could be very dangerous. As I began to slide down the river sideways, my panic increased and I did the unthinkable. I saw the boulder I mentioned and tried to make a large step in an attempt to reach it and pull myself out. The laws of physics suddenly took over and I went totally submerged in the current. I jumped up and tried to reach the rock again and missed and went back under the water. I jumped up and tried to reach the bolder again but missed due to the current pulling me downstream. I found myself under the water a second time. The tail waters of the dam upstream are fairly cold to sustain a trout population and I could not catch my breath. I had been under water twice and knew if I couldn't reach the boulder the next time, I might not get another chance. I struggled and pushed up with everything I had and finally reached the boulder and was able to pull myself out of the river's current.

As humans we have a tendency to venture into place where we should not go. We go to places in our mind and in our emotions, and look at things we should never have seen. We go to the places where Christians do not belong and perhaps do not realize the danger this can cause in our relationship with the Lord. King David violated a number of these principles when he looked at Bathsheba as she bathed on her roof. Instead of keeping both feet on solid ground he took another man's wife and eventually had her husband put in a situation where his death would be inevitable. He did this in attempt to cover up his sin. We know how the story ended, and the severe consequences that King David experienced both in his relationship with the Lord and with his family. You can read the full account in 2 Samuel in Chapters 11 and 12. Let me encourage you to maintain your integrity and not venture into areas that will cause terrible harm to your relationship with Christ and cause pain and disappointment to your family and friends. Remember that forgiveness is always available from Jesus, but the situation you have caused may not be repairable. Keep your eyes focused on Christ alone!

Dear Lord, Help me to keep myself pure and unstained by the world and its ungodly influences. Help me to know that friendship with the world and its values is not healthy to my relationship with You. In Jesus Name, Amen.

CHAPTER 22

The Adventure

"By faith Abraham, when he was called, obeyed by going out...and he went out, not knowing where he was going."

— Hebrews 11:8 NASB

FISHERMEN ALWAYS HAVE A FEELING of excitement and anticipation of finding a new place to fish. I always like going the extra mile where I see no signs of other fishermen, and then I reasonably expect that these fish have not been fished a lot. If that be true, one could also reasonably expect to find bigger and less finicky fish. There is also a sense of adventure when you find yourself alone with no one to rely on or talk to. You look around and all you see is woods and water. However, the downside is that if something were to happen, there is no one to help you. There is this sense of isolation and perhaps some very healthy concern, but the excitement of feeling that bend on the end of your fly rod overrides these concerns. Now by chance I make this trip with a trusted friend, I feel much more comfortable. I know I have someone to rely on in the event of an emergency or to get advice concerning which way to go or which fly to use.

My wife and I have led many mission trips to El Salvador under a missionary that resides there. We have a reputation of going where other teams from America don't feel comfortable going. For me, as the team leader, I want to go farther because the people in these far reaching areas have not heard of the love of Jesus as often, if at all, as the closer communities. Going to a third world country can take us out of our comfort zone, and going even farther can make us feel extremely uncomfortable. We don't go into these places alone but have the missionary, one of his trusted associates or a 'national' as they are called along with us. The nationals live in the country we are visiting. We have these 'trusted' individuals to help us and guide us along. While we are out of our comfort zone, we know we are not alone.

Perhaps God has been speaking to you about becoming part of a new endeavor. Maybe your church is sponsoring a mission trip outside of the United States and you have never done that. Maybe you have never been out of your home state. One Sunday your pastor or team leader was speaking about a trip they were planning or had been on. As they were showing the pictures and sharing what God had done on the trip, you felt a stirring in your heart that maybe God was speaking to you about going. Fear then grips your heart as the tug of war began between your desire to go and your fear of being totally out of your comfort zone. Maybe God is asking you to be a part of a ministry in your church, such as the men's or women's ministry, or working with children or teaching a Sunday School class. Jesus asked Peter to step out of his boat out and maybe He is asking you to step out of yours. This was totally out of Peter's comfort zone and something he had never done before. But he trusted Jesus and he did walk on water! You are thinking now that whatever it is that God is speaking to me about is way out of my comfort zone. Of course it is. If it wasn't, we wouldn't really need to trust Jesus to help us, would we? When you step out, Jesus will be there to take you by the hand and walk beside you, as He did Peter. Not only will it strengthen your faith, you will find that you will be a blessing to others as you allow God to use you. What is He asking you to do today?

Dear Lord, If you are calling me to a work for You, please give me the courage to step out of the security of my boat and comfort zone to follow You. I know You will never leave me nor forsake me. I want to be obedient to Your calling. In Jesus Name, Amen.

CHAPTER 23
The Flushing

"Watch yourselves, that you do not lose what we have accomplished, but that you may receive a full reward."

— 2 John 1:8 NASB

One beautiful fall day I was fly fishing the lower Savage River in western Maryland. This particular river is a Trophy Trout Management area for Brown and Brook trout. It is the tail water of the Savage River Dam which extends approximately 4.5 miles downstream from the dam. It is a beautiful combination of rocks, boulders, sunken logs with pools and runs throughout its length which makes it a perfect trout river. It has lots of structure for the fish to survive in and multiple hatches throughout the year which makes it a fly fisherman's dream river.

I was fishing this one particular pool that was created in front of a very large boulder and I noticed lots of leaves floating through the water. It was during the fall of the year so I didn't pay much attention to them. Eventually the floating and submerged leaves were being caught on my fly on every cast. I looked around to see what was causing this enormous amount of leaves to float past me. Much to my astonishment, all the boulders and rocks that were spaced through the river and some that I had even walked on were all gone. All I could see was a flat, fast moving and quickly rising river coming straight at me. I had been so focused on perfecting my cast around the currents in front of the boulder that I hadn't noticed the rising river. I knew I needed to make a hasty exit from the river. This part of the river had very thick underbrush along the banks and easy quick exits are not always possible. In my urgency I was able to punch my way through the brush and headed out of the river.

I headed back to my van and by that time the river was very high and the current extremely powerful. Anyone caught in the river at that time would have been swept downstream quickly had he not acted quickly as I did. It turned out to be a normal 'flushing' of the river that is done during the fall and spring to flush the river of debris and leaves. Unfortunately there is not a siren or any kind of warning when that takes place.

As Christians, we always have to be on guard as the enemy is looking for a way to trip us up and cause us to sin. The temptation is often subtle and without much fanfare but always deadly. Much like the river, it happens when we let our guard down and it sneaks up on us. If we are caught off guard, the results can be catastrophic. It has been said that a hole the size of a quarter could sink a battleship. Water will come in very slowly at first and no one will even notice. Eventually the ship becomes sluggish and hard to steer. When the captain tries to steer away from the reef to avoid ripping the hull open and sinking the ship it is too late. Destruction now is inevitable. I want to encourage Christians not to compromise on our values and to stay away from activities that we should not be involved in. It may appear harmless at first, and no apparent damage has been done, but hurt and pain may not be far away. Unlike the river rising, the Holy Spirit will give us the warning we need, but it's up to us if we will listen. Is God speaking to you today about being on guard against something?

Dear Lord, Help me to stay close to You so I am aware of any subtle attempts to compromise my integrity. I understand that any sin, regardless of how small I may think it is, could be used by the enemy to gain a stronghold in my heart. I want You to be glorified in all that I do and say. In Jesus Name, Amen.

CHAPTER 24
The Whiff

"But each one is tempted when he is carried away and enticed by his own lust."

— JAMES 1:14 NASB

I AM AN AVID USER of scents and lures when hunting the whitetail deer. However, I have seen some work and seen some not work. I have seen deer walk right over a scent line that I had recently put down with their nose to the ground and never bothered to follow it. I do recall a scent line I had put down during the early season bow hunt. It was more of a curiosity lure for that time of year along an old logging road. In order to bring any deer right below my stand I had to lay it around several trees in a rather curved trail. I saw the deer walking down the logging road, hit the scent trail and began to follow it exactly as I had laid it down. She was around forty yards out and suddenly stopped. She stood there for the longest time almost as if she was frozen. Then as calmly as she had walked in, she turned around and walked away. She obviously thought that she was following a familiar scent but then realized something wasn't quite right. Her instincts probably saved her life that evening.

There was another time from that same stand when I had a nice six point buck come in to the sound of some grunts and antler rattling. He came in quickly but didn't offer a good shot and started to walk away. Suddenly, his nose went up in the air and smelled the buck lure I had on a cotton ball. He turned around and came back and offered me a nice shot. He ended up in my freezer that evening.

In another scenario I had some buck lure on a limb trying to catch a buck cruising by but instead had a doe come in early that morning. She was coming in cautiously when she suddenly stopped outside the shooting lane. She put her nose high in the air and caught a whiff of the lure. She sensed something wasn't quite right and turned around and trotted off. As with the other doe, her instincts probably saved her life that morning.

What did these does have in common? They did what comes naturally to them. They have noses that are trained to smell, and these scents are transmitted to their brain. After discerning these smells, they determine whether it is safe to proceed or to run the other way. Those that listen to their instincts live to see another day. The does mentioned in the previous stories had no idea how close they came to being in my freezer. What they did know was that something wasn't right, and to avoid danger they turned and ran.

We are told in the Bible that a characteristic of a mature man or woman of God is one "...who because of practice have their senses trained to discern good and evil." Hebrews 5:14 NASB. We need to strive to read our Bible and pray so that we may become the mature Christian in order to discern the difference between good and evil. It is not always apparent. The devil would never come with a temptation that is ugly and disgusting. We would never be tempted by that no more than a deer would be tempted by an unnatural odor in the woods. Instead he will come with something attractive and alluring and unless we have our senses trained, we may fall into his trap. Our choices, as the deer's, can determine whether we live or die. A pounding in our heart or a disturbance in our spirit may be the warning sign that God is giving us to avoid the danger that lurks waiting to destroy us. We must always stay alert!

Dear Lord, Help me to be aware of lures and enticements that will lead me away from You. I realize that if I follow these I will hurt myself spiritually and may cause deep hurts in those that I love. In Jesus Name, Amen.

CHAPTER 25

The Sanctuary

"You are my hiding place, You preserve me from trouble."

— Psalm 32:7 NASB

It is no surprise that in the world of the forest the animals have places where they can go and feel safe. Turkeys roost in trees at night to get above the predators that roam the forest at nighttime. Turkeys will also fly up to the treetops during the day to get away from daytime predators. Unfortunately, hen turkeys with their poults do not have a sanctuary to fly to but rather stay with their young ones until they can fly up on their own. Their world becomes a dangerous place during this time.

We have an area where we hunt that is thick with mountain laurel that deer use as a sanctuary. It is thick and gnarly and the only way through it is to navigate the very narrow deer trails. This sanctuary is also situated on a very steep hillside giving the deer a commanding view of what comes and goes through their world. Nothing will enter or leave without their knowing it. During the winter, the snow reveals the most concentrated amount of deer tracks in the entire area where we hunt, thus the sanctuary is used heavily for a sanctuary throughout the year. The mountain laurel is so thick that a hunter could not even get a shot off if he did see a deer fleeing. Other forest animals also have sanctuaries where they flee when trouble is approaching. Squirrels have their trees, chipmunks and minks have holes to flee into and foxes have their dens but the common denominator is that they all have safe havens to go when danger come looking for them. Without their sanctuaries, these animals would certainly live in fear when their predator would be on the prowl.

Everyone, including animals, need a place they can flee to when danger comes. A place to feel safe until the danger passes by. As humans, we are faced with many situations that can feel overwhelming at times. People often reach out for God in these times of crisis, but in many cases they may not know the Lord personally and therefore do not know where or how to find Him. These overwhelming times of crisis can quickly break a person's spirit and often destroys them.

It doesn't have to be that way for Christians. The Bible often tells us that God is our sanctuary and a safe haven. We should establish a regular place of prayer, praise and reading God's Word so we know that we have a place of refuge. We are not exempt from life as it throws things at us that often take us completely off guard. There are wounds that cut deep into our hearts from spouses and trusted friends. Perhaps it comes in the form of an unexpected layoff, death of a family member or deadly illness. We become so paralyzed emotionally that we don't even know how to respond or what to say. Life can be tough, but we know that we have a God that loves us and a sanctuary where He can be found. Are you facing an overwhelming challenge today? He is waiting for you in your sanctuary to pour your heart out to Him. When you do, He will wrap His arms around you and you will feel His never ending love.

Dear Lord, When trouble comes into my life, please help me to remember that You are the One that will provide a shelter during the storm. You will comfort and strengthen me and hide me until trouble passes by. In Jesus Name, Amen.

CHAPTER 26

Weapon Ready?

> Beloved, do not believe every spirit, but test the spirits to see whether they are from God, because many false prophets have gone out into the world."
>
> — I John 4:1 NASB

My goal when I am hunting, regardless of weapon, is to make a clean, efficient shot that results in a quick, clean kill. I have any archery range in the backyard complete with a ladderstand that measures twenty yards from the 3-D target. I spend many hours practicing shooting and making sure my form is good so my arrow flies true to the kill zone of the deer. I need to be confident that when I touch the trigger on the release that I have done all I can do to prepare for that moment.

I also love to turkey hunt with my 12 gauge shotgun. I spend a lot of range time determining the pattern that my current combination of gun, choke and shot size will be when the shot hits the turkey. I killed a turkey this year with that set up, and the turkey dropped on the spot at twenty five yards. I have confidence that when I pull the trigger, assuming I aim correctly, the shot is going to do the job.

I also rifle hunt and use a 30.06 with a 150 grain bullet. I spend range time each year to be sure nothing has changed since last year and the scope has not been bumped. I double check the accuracy at 100 yards, and I am happy when I can consistently put all the bullets within a three to four inch bullseye. I am then confident that my weapon will place the bullet where it needs to be to make that clean, efficient shot.

The world as we know it is changing and Christian values are falling like dominos. Even mainline churches are giving in to be politically correct and changing their theology that has been the cornerstone of their tenants of faith for many, many years. This devotional is not about the world of politics but about being diligent "...to present yourself approved to God a workman who does not need to be ashamed, accurately handling the word of truth." 2 Timothy 2:15 NASB. What if Bill who sits with you at lunch, suddenly turns to you and asks, "Hey Fred, what does the Bible say about all this?" Or maybe you are on a hunting trip with a friend and he knows you are a Christian. Suddenly he turns to you and without hesitation he asks about all this salvation stuff. His wife has been talking to him about it and he is searching. How do you respond? This is the moment for which you have been waiting. So in a loving and a non- condemning way you explain what the Bible states.

We need to remember that it is not necessary to convince anyone of the truth if he disagrees with what we share with him from the Bible. That is the function and purpose of the Holy Spirit who will "...convince the world concerning sin, and righteousness and judgement." John 16:8 NASB. The key here is to have our spiritual weapon ready and to be prepared to know how to use it. We need to know what the Word of God says. In our devotional time we need to practice, practice and practice so we are confident in our ability to use the Word of God and know it will do exactly what it says it will do in the hearts and lives of our family and friends.

Dear Lord, Help me to know Your Word and to properly use it during these last days. As our world continues to turn away from God, I want to be ready to share Your Word with my family and friends so they will know the truth. In Jesus Name, Amen.

CHAPTER 27
Bread Crumbs

"Make me know your ways, O Lord,
Teach me your paths."

— Psalm 25:4 NASB

Not sure about you, but I really dislike getting lost in the woods. Sometimes it happens and it can be an unnerving situation, especially when no one knows at that time we are lost. Just a side note, you should let your family or friends know where you are going in the woods and what time you expect to be back and always carry a cell phone. We remember the story of Hansel and Gretel leaving bread crumbs in the woods so they could find their way back. As good as that idea may have seemed at the moment, it didn't work out very well for them. Fortunately that story did have a happy ending. For many years we relied on a map and compass to get us through unfamiliar woods. Today's topographic maps show us with contour lines where the hilly and steep areas are as well as the roads, rivers, lakes, plateaus and other physical characteristics that help us to navigate through the woods. At the very least every hunter should have one of these maps with him at all times.

With the introduction of the GPS (Global Positioning Device) navigating through the woods has become much easier. They have topographical maps that can actually be loaded into these devices so your exact location can be pinpointed with amazing accuracy. Your global coordinates are being updated constantly so in the event of an accident, you can call in your position to the emergency rescue personnel so they will know your exact location. You can select a location with its known coordinates even before leaving your home and set your GPS to take you to the exact spot. Or you can log in a place where you have been and set the GPS to take you back to that particular spot. In short, the GPS has revolutionized our ability to go anywhere using satellite tracking and then to find our way back. Make sure you pack extra batteries when you are relying on a GPS to get you around. You can also leave bread crumbs on your GPS to navigate from one point to another and unlike the ones used by Hansel and Gretel, these are electronically saved. The bottom line in all of this is when I need guidance in the woods and places that I am not familiar with, I can trust my GPS to get me there and back. I feel comfortable in unfamiliar territory knowing I am not left to navigate on my own.

I have found that navigating through life has its own hazards as well, and I have had my share of bruises and even a few major collisions along the way, and I'm sure you have too. The Bible states, "Your word is a lamp to my feet, and a light to my path." Psalm 119:105 NASB. When I walk to my stand in the darkness I need a light so I don't trip and hurt myself. If I need a lamp to walk in this life to avoid hurting myself or others, then the Word of God will give us that light. I can read what God expects of me and what is sinful and hurtful to me or others. His Word encourages me to participate in good deeds so I can reflect the love of my Savior that is living in me. The best part of all is that the Bible is not powered by batteries and a satellite, but by God himself who desires to give us guidance. He is always waiting with open arms to take us by the hand and lead us through the unexpected twists and turns, but also our day to day living so we stay on the right path. Need direction? Open up the Bible and you may be surprised how much direction your life will have.

Dear Lord, Please teach me from Your Word how You want me to live. I need You to give me direction so I take the path You desire for me. In Jesus Name, Amen

CHAPTER 28

The Fall

"Pride goes before destruction. And a haughty spirit before stumbling."

— Proverbs 16:18 NASB

ONE OF THE GREATEST HUNTS I have ever had was this past spring when I took a nice two year old gobbler. After talking turkey with him for awhile, he came out of the woods to my left in full strut. He was magnificent looking. His chest and body were all puffed out as he told the hen decoys, "Hey, look at me, aren't I just the best looking gobbler you have ever seen?" He certainly thought he was the top turkey that morning. He came across the field for thirty yards still in full strut trying to impress the girls and probably trying to intimidate the Jake decoy I had set out with the hens. Moments after he reached the decoys he was on the ground, a victim of #6 shot from a 12 gauge shotgun at twenty five yards. I had never seen a gobbler come in full strut like that before and it was exhilarating. The Bible states that pride goes before a fall, and if that applies to the animal world as well then this was a perfect example. Peter, the great disciple had with great pride, told Jesus that even if everyone deserted Him in those final moments, he would not. He would stand with him no matter what. As the Bible relates, Peter not only denied Jesus, but he did it three times, as Jesus had foretold him.

Pride can manifest itself in many ways and often times very subtly. Sometimes we are not openly aware that we are guilty of it. In the hunting and fishing realm, we often brag about the biggest fish, the biggest buck and how far the shot was, all the while we are telling people what great hunters or fisherman we are. Sometimes there is a fine line between being excited and sharing that adventure with our family and friends and saying that," If you did what I did, you could be successful too."

Sometimes it has to do with our toys. The new car, the new gun, bass boat, four wheeler and on and on we go. Look what I have! It's not wrong to have our toys, but it's the attitude in which we display them to the world. Pride can even manifest itself in our attitude towards others within the church. Maybe we are asked to lead a Sunday School class or a Bible study and we start to think that we must be pretty spiritual to be asked to do this. Or we refuse to volunteer at the local mission because it has all those kind of people down there. We can take an attitude of favoritism because we tithe and attend church every time it is open.

I know a very humble and successful local businessman who is a Christian. He has a beautiful lakeside home with a nice boat and all the amenities. No one would ever be aware of his wealth by talking to him. If he bought a new boat no one would ever know it. He is one of the most humble persons I know. He has taken many mission trips to third world countries and has been extremely generous with his time and resources to help those less fortunate, both here and abroad. We are told in the Bible that "A man's pride will bring him low, But a humble spirit will obtain honor." Proverbs 29:23 NASB and "Let another man praise you, and not your own mouth; A stranger, and not your own lips." Proverbs 27:12 NASB. We should take some time to be alone with God and ask Him to point out any areas of our lives that have pride surrounding them. And ask Him to help us become more humble.

Dear Lord, Help me to be humble in all that I do and say. While I may be successful in areas of my life, may I ever give You praise for the desires and abilities You have given me. Help me to remember that my life is not about me, but about You living in Me. In Jesus Name, Amen.

CHAPTER 29

Watchful

> "For this reason you also must be ready; for the Son of Man is coming at an hour when you do not think He will."
>
> — Matthew 24:44 NASB

Technology has come a long way in the hunting community. I remember the early version of the trail camera, however it wasn't even a camera but a trail timer and it was pretty basic. It was a piece of thread strung between two trees along a supposed deer trail. The one end of the string was attached to a detachable plastic clip that was in turn attached to a small housing that contained a clock. When the deer, or other animal walked down the trail would push against the thread and break it, it would pull the clip out of the housing and stop the clock. That would tell you what time the thread was broken and the direction of the thread that was hanging indicated which direction the culprit was heading. Like I said, it was pretty basic. This was by design only a single event timer and had to be reset each time it was triggered. It was not really time effective, and didn't work all that well either. At least mine didn't.

Now hunters have trail cameras with all the bells and whistles one could possibly think of. Today's cameras records not only the picture of what triggered the event, but the time, date and even the moon phase The more sophisticated hunter can now receive trail cam pictures via satellite transmitted to his computer without leaving the comfort of his own home. We have come a long way since the thread strung between two trees! Now we know the exact time and dates that the deer are coming under your stand and we can plan to be there and be ready to take the shot.

There is another occurrence that is coming, but we cannot pinpoint the day or the time when it will happen. And because we don't know the exact time or day, the question one would ask is how then could we possibly be ready. Jesus said in the Bible that He will be coming back to this earth to receive His church. He also said that no one will know the date or the time and the only way to be ready is to stay ready. Although some have tried, there is no technology that can give us this information. I have experienced this lack of knowing exactly when during turkey hunting. I have heard a gobbler and even talked back and forth to him when suddenly he goes quiet. So I start to think is he coming in quietly or is he following another hen somewhere. I normally assume he is coming quietly, and get my gun ready and sit there like a statue, ready to shoot if he comes, but not knowing when or if but I have to be ready in the event he does. I will only have one chance if he is coming, because if I relax like he is not coming, he does and I am not ready and miss an opportunity.

We must be ready every moment as we will have only one chance to be ready for His coming. It will happen according to the Bible, "...in a moment, in the twinkling of an eye, at the last trumpet; for the trumpet will sound..." I Corinthians 15:52 NASB. How will He find us? Will we be found obedient and faithful or just the opposite? Will we be found lukewarm or will our hearts be steadfast by following Christ? Will we hear the words, "Well done, good and faithful servant." Matthew 25:23 NIV. Take a moment and ask God that if Jesus would return today are there some areas of your life that you should have changed. If there are, ask Him for help and tell Him that you want to be found ready.

Dear Lord, I eagerly await Your return to take me home to be with You forever. As I do not know the time or day when You will return may I be found ready with my hope fixed on You. In Jesus Name, Amen

CHAPTER 30

Wounded

〜

"Therefore repent and return, so that your sins may be wiped away, in order that times of refreshing my come from the presence of the Lord."

—Acts 3:19 NASB

I'M NOT SURE IF YOU feel the same way I do about hunting but I take it pretty seriously. I don't mean I don't have fun or go around with a frown all the time. If it wasn't fun I wouldn't do it. I love to hunt. I love the preparation and anticipation and everything about it. What I do mean is that when I shoot at an animal I expect the animal to go down. I spend hours in preparation on the range for that moment. I respect the animal that I hunt and want to be a responsible hunter by making a quick, clean and efficient kill shot. I generally practice with my bow two or three days a week, take several sessions with the shotgun making sure it patterns well for turkeys, and usually a session with the 30.06 to make sure it is still sighted in from the previous year.

 I regret having to say this, but I have on rare occasion wounded a deer and have been unable to locate it. Not from a lack of searching because I will spend hours looking and have even gone back the next day to try and pick up any trail. But sometimes the inevitable happens and it cannot be found. It's at this point that I take my hunting very seriously. I feel like a failure, and am ashamed and disappointed in myself. Afterward I don't even want to talk about it nor even talk about hunting with anyone. I am thinking about all the practice and all the preparation and for what? I blew it. I just want to go home and hide and thoughts of never going hunting again enter my head. Eventually I work through it and move forward but it takes time. It does make me more determined to learn from my mistakes and to take steps to ensure that never happens again.

Sometimes the same scenario happens in our spiritual lives, but in that arena it becomes much more serious because human lives are affected by our actions. We have a tendency to make mistakes which involve sinful actions that can and do deeply hurt the ones we love. These events may be promises not kept and trust that is broken and more serious issues like infidelity. And we ask ourselves, "How did this happen? How could I have hurt the ones I love so deeply and now what do I do?" We may feel ashamed, humiliated and disappointed. We may feel unworthy of anyone's love, including God's. You may feel unworthy to be called a Christian and find yourself not wanting to read your Bible or pray. You may feel like the hunter, what's the point, I blew it! You do everything you are supposed to but it still happened.

You need to know that God still loves you and while He takes sin very seriously, He still offers forgiveness for anything you may have done. If you are truly sorry for what has happened you may have trouble forgiving yourself. Others may have trouble forgiving you as well. It is at that point that you are in a dark spot and need help walking out. May I recommend seeking out your pastor or the most godly, trusted person you know to share what has happened. In addition, however, there is no easy solution for the lives that were hurt. Those solutions may be a part of the consequences for our actions. Take one day at a time, the process may be slow but there is definitely hope and forgiveness found in Christ.

Dear Lord, Please forgive me for the hurt and pain I have caused those I love. I humbly ask for Your help to bring me back to a place of forgiveness and restoration. Please heal those hearts I broke by my actions. In Jesus Name, Amen.

For additional copies of this book, go to Amazon.com

Made in the USA
Columbia, SC
14 November 2017